The Big Book for Peace

Edited by Ann Durell and Marilyn Sachs
Designed by Jane Byers Bierhorst

Dutton Children's Books › NEW YORK

THE BIG BOOK FOR
P · E · A · C · E

WRITTEN BY

Lloyd Alexander · Natalie Babbitt
John Bierhorst · Jean Fritz · Jean Craighead George
Thacher Hurd · Steven Kellogg · Myra Cohn Livingston
Lois Lowry · Milton Meltzer · Katherine Paterson
Marilyn Sachs · Yoshiko Uchida · Mildred Pitts Walter
Nancy Willard · Charlotte Zolotow

ILLUSTRATED BY

Jon Agee · Thomas B. Allen · Barbara Cooney
Diane and Leo Dillon · Leonard Everett Fisher
Thacher Hurd · Trina Schart Hyman · Steven Kellogg
Jerry Pinkney · Ted Rand · Allen Say · Maurice Sendak
Ben Shecter · Marc Simont · Teri Sloat
Paul O. Zelinsky · Dirk Zimmer

Library of Congress Cataloging-in-Publication Data

The big book for peace / edited by Ann Durell and Marilyn Sachs;
written by Lloyd Alexander . . . [et al.]; illustrated by
Thomas B. Allen . . . [et al.]—1st ed.
p.   cm.
Summary: The wisdom of peace and the absurdity of fighting are
demonstrated in seventeen stories and poems by outstanding authors
of today such as Jean Fritz, Milton Meltzer, and Nancy Willard,
illustrated by famous illustrators such as Paul Zelinsky,
the Dillons, and Maurice Sendak.
ISBN 0-525-44605-2
1. Peace—Literary collections.   2. Children's literature, American.
[1. Peace—Literary collections.]   I. Durell, Ann.
II. Sachs, Marilyn.   III. Alexander, Lloyd.
IV. Allen, Thomas B. (Thomas Burt), date, ill.
PZ5.B445   1990   810.8′0358—dc20
[Fic]   89-37595   CIP   AC

Published in the United States by Dutton Children's Books,
a division of Penguin Books USA Inc.
First Edition
10 9 8 7 6 5 4 3 2 1

INTRODUCTION

Peace is important. Anyone who has ever been hurt in a quarrel or a fight or watched TV news or read a newspaper knows that. And with the possibility of nuclear war still present, world peace continues to be crucial to everyone on this planet.

So this is an important book. It looks at the idea of peace in many different ways. In fantasy tales and present-day stories, some funny and some serious. In true incidents, some that happened in the past and some that are happening right now. In poems, pictures, and even a song.

All of us who have worked together on it invite all of you who will be reading it to join us in celebrating peace. We hope the book will give you new ways to think and talk about peace. We hope that you will write your own stories and poems about peace, draw your own pictures, and sing your own songs. Above all, we hope you will help us to spread the word, the big word—PEACE—to others.

Ann Durell and Marilyn Sachs
Editors

Contents

The Big Book for Peace

The Dream

by Steven Kellogg

If everyone has the same dream,

it might come true.

A PEACEABLE KINGDOM.

The Two Brothers

by Lloyd Alexander

illustrated by Dirk Zimmer

There once were two brothers, Ninniaw and Pebbiaw, whose father had willed his small kingdom to be shared equally between them. However, since there was only one castle, the question arose: Which twin should keep it and which leave and build another?

"Dear brother Pebbiaw," said Ninniaw, "I wouldn't dream of putting you to such trouble. Let us, above all, be at peace with each other. You shall stay here and I shall build a new castle."

"Dear brother Ninniaw," said Pebbiaw, "that's kind and thoughtful of you, as to be expected from a generous-hearted, loving brother. Yes, by all means, let us be at peace. But you must stay. I shall be the one to move."

So they talked back and forth, each concerned for the other's comfort and well-being, until at last they agreed: Neither should keep the castle. Instead, each would build his own. The old stronghold was to be torn down, and whatever could be used from it would be divided.

Having come to such a wise and fair decision, they clasped hands on it and embraced, as fond as any brothers could ever be.

The two then set about building their strongholds, little more than a stone's throw apart.

"Dear brother," said Ninniaw, when the castles were finished, "those are fine, handsome walls you've put up, very solid indeed. I don't question your judgment, but why did you need to build them so high?"

"For your protection, dear brother," said Pebbiaw. "The world, alas, is full of wicked folk. Should anyone attack you, they'll have to deal with me first."

"How right you are, dear brother," said Ninniaw. "And I can do no less for you."

So Ninniaw commanded his own walls and towers be raised to the height of Pebbiaw's. This done, Ninniaw invited Pebbiaw to a feast in the great hall.

There, spread out on long tables, were cutlets of roast venison—and quail, partridge, and pheasant by the hundreds; for Ninniaw had sent his foresters to hunt and snare the choicest game in his woods.

"Dear brother," cried Pebbiaw, having stuffed himself as full as he could, "there's never been such a feast in all my memory! What a joy to have a brother whose hands are as open as his heart is kind!"

"Dear brother," answered Ninniaw, "how good of you to give high praise to such lowly offerings. Once my kitchen is in better order, you shall have dainties to match my affection for you."

The two princes embraced and wished each other a fond good night.

But Pebbiaw went back to his castle grumbling along the way, "Affection for his own good opinion of himself is what I call it. He's trying to outshine me again. Well, I'll show him dainties!"

And so Pebbiaw, in turn, spread out a feast for Ninniaw. The tables groaned under even more lavish fare, for Pebbiaw had ordered his gamekeepers to seek out the rarest delicacies. The platters were heaped high, not only with quail and pheasant, but larks and linnets surrounded by their eggs, boiled, coddled, and poached; and fish of every sort, broiled and seasoned to perfection.

When Ninniaw blinked in amazement at the endless courses, Pebbiaw shrugged and said, "Dear brother, forgive me. My modest board has little worth your notice or that shows my esteem for you. Next time, I promise you shall be better served."

From then on, hardly a day went by without the two brothers visiting each other. And each feast was always more splendid than the last, with Ninniaw and Pebbiaw striving to outdo each other no matter what the cost.

After a time, however, seeing his provisions dwindle, Ninniaw muttered to himself, "What a greedy pig that brother of mine is! He's going to eat me out of house and home!"

And so he stopped inviting his brother to dinner or, indeed, any other meal.

Pebbiaw, for his part, frowning at the nearly bare shelves of his larder, grumbled, "That Ninniaw has a bottomless pit for a stomach. Wretch! He'd be delighted if I beggared myself feeding him."

And Pebbiaw, likewise, no longer invited his brother to share his hospitality.

The two brothers not only stopped dining together, they soon barely spoke to each other.

Then one day Ninniaw noticed that Pebbiaw had increased the number of archers and spearmen keeping watch on his ramparts.

Ninniaw could hardly let this pass unremarked. When he asked the reason, Pebbiaw replied, "These are hard times, Brother, with more than one rascal at large in the world. Better to be alert and ready for whatever may befall."

"You were always prudent, Brother," said Ninniaw. "I admire you for it. But those bowmen of yours are hot-headed fellows. What if some day, for the sport of it or by accident, they let fly a volley of arrows at my guards?"

"That will not happen, Brother," Pebbiaw assured him. "You have my word on it."

Even so, the next day Ninniaw set about raising the height of his walls.

When Pebbiaw came hotfooting over in indignation, demanding to know why, Ninniaw told him, "You and I are brothers and so have nothing to fear from each other. Can you say as much for your warriors?"

"True," said Pebbiaw, "but now your men are so high they could, out of sheer mischief, shower spears into my courtyard."

And Pebbiaw, in turn, raised his battlements higher than those of Ninniaw.

Ninniaw first thought of building his own walls even higher. Then he decided against it.

"That brother of mine was always a pigheaded fool," he said to himself. "If I raise my walls, he'll only do the same. No, I shall follow a shrewder plan."

The next day, Ninniaw ordered a few of his warriors to climb the trees overlooking Pebbiaw's castle and keep close watch. This way, he told himself, he would learn whatever new folly his brother might be up to, and put an end to it before it got out of hand.

The following morning, however, Ninniaw woke to the sound of chopping. Hurrying to his wall, he saw Pebbiaw's woodcutters felling the trees encircling his castle.

When he hastily rode over to ask his brother the reason, Pebbiaw sighed and shook his head, saying, "Ah, Brother, the times are troubled. Who can tell when some band of ruffians might take it into their heads to spy upon us and attack me? Better to have a clearing around my stronghold, so no one can come upon me unawares."

"You are right, Brother," Ninniaw answered agreeably. "For a moment, I feared you might have lost your trust in our affection. But I see now that your idea is marvelously sensible."

So Ninniaw in turn ordered his woodcutters to cut down the trees around his stronghold. But when he rode out to oversee the work, he glimpsed Pebbiaw watching and, with him, a band of warriors.

"Why, Brother, what is this?" called Ninniaw. "Do you

mean to hunt? Had you told me, I would have gone with you."

"No, Brother, I do not hunt," replied Pebbiaw in a surly tone. "I find this as good a time as any to settle our boundaries."

"Excellent thought," said Ninniaw, glaring. "It will be an easy matter. Since we share alike, our boundary should be set exactly here, halfway between our castles."

"Well and good," said Pebbiaw, striding past his brother, "but you misjudge your distance by half a dozen yards. It should be—here."

"What, Brother, do you say I have no eye for measurement?" retorted Ninniaw.

"On the contrary, Brother," Pebbiaw returned. "You have a sharp eye when it comes to looking out for yourself. Small wonder you want such a boundary, since it carves a fat slice out of my land."

"That stumpy chicken-walk?" cried Ninniaw. "Your land isn't worth carving."

"Back up, then!" shouted Pebbiaw. "Move closer into that scabby rat-run of yours and mark the boundary where it should be."

"So I do!" shouted Ninniaw, drawing his sword and slashing a line in the dirt. "I mark it here!"

"And I mark it there!" cried Pebbiaw, snatching out his own sword and pointing to a spot some distance beyond Ninniaw.

Seeing the brothers with drawn blades and supposing their leader to be in danger, Pebbiaw's warriors raced forward. Ninniaw, certain his brother had betrayed him, galloped for dear life toward his castle, with Pebbiaw and the warriors brandishing their weapons in hot pursuit.

Seeing Ninniaw beset, the guards on his castle walls raised the alarm, and his war band burst through the gates to engage Pebbiaw and his men. The latter, finding themselves outnumbered, shouted for reinforcements. And so an even larger war band rode from Pebbiaw's castle, while another from Ninniaw's stronghold galloped to stand against them.

The battle was so quickly and hotly joined that neither side could withdraw. By the time Ninniaw and Pebbiaw brought their warriors, and themselves, to their senses, the gates of both castles had been shattered, the halls and chambers set ablaze, and nothing remained but two piles of fire-blackened stones.

Ninniaw and Pebbiaw could only stare, open-mouthed and dumbstruck, hardly able to believe their eyes.

"Brother," Ninniaw said at last, "I fear your castle has been somewhat damaged."

"To say the least of it," muttered Pebbiaw. "And so has yours."

They stood awhile, still befuddled by what had happened.

Finally, saying no more, they turned away and trudged

back to their heaps of rubble, shaking their heads, each wondering how the other could have been so remarkably dim-witted.

There Is an Island

by Jean Fritz

illustrated by Teri Sloat

Once long ago in the far, far north, there lived a giant who had such long legs that he could cross from one continent to another in a single step. So one day he put his left leg firmly on the coast of Siberia. Then he stretched his right leg—and stretched and stretched it until his foot came down on North America. And there he was straddling the Bering Sea! Below

him he saw the sea—big but empty. What it needed was an island. So reaching down, the giant scooped up a handful of mud from the bottom of the sea and began squeezing the water out of it. He squeezed and squeezed until it was as dry as any island could be. Then he planted it in the emptiness. Not in the middle. No, he placed it closer to his left leg, close to Siberia. Later the island was called St. Lawrence Island, but the people who live there have always called it *Sivuqaq,* which in their language means "squeezed dry."

The people in the "squeezed dry" place are Yupik Eskimos. And although their island belongs to America, they live so close to Siberian Yupiks that they speak the same language, share the same customs, and often have the same names. Over the years they have visited back and forth as if they were part of one big family. They have sung together, hunted together, danced together, and traded together—American chewing tobacco and walrus hides in return for reindeer pants, alder bark, and wolf-skin ruffs.

And every June and July, the men from St. Lawrence and the men from Siberia would get together to race and wrestle with each other. The races started as soon as the people from Siberia arrived in Gambell, the town perched on the tip of the island closest to Siberia. The men ran around a circular track, around and around, until one by one they had to drop out, and at last only the winner was left.

Then a St. Lawrence man took off his parka and went to the center of the circle and squatted. This meant that it was time for wrestling and he took on anyone who challenged him. One by one, they entered the ring. But as soon as a man was knocked down, he had to quit. The champion was the last one left on his feet.

All year the men trained for this event, each man wanting to prove his strength. The training for the competition was so fierce that one might expect fights to break out. But they didn't. The people of St. Lawrence honored peace above all else, and the elders on the island made sure that peace was kept. The elders were used to settling arguments whenever they occurred, winter or summer. They ordered the contestants to wrestle or vie with each other in lifting heavy rocks, and soon arguments were forgotten and hasty words forgiven.

It was the same during the competition when the Siberians were there. If tempers began to get out of hand, the elders had only to say, "Enough!" So everyone stayed in good spirits, and at the end of the contests, all were ready for the feasting and fun to begin. They played games, ate and danced together—men and women, boys and girls. And they sang. Long, long into the summer twilight they sang the old songs they all knew.

The elders were considered the wisest and most important people on the island. After all, they were the ones who had "seen the sun first" and welcomed it back most often. What

could be more special than that? So the elders were the ones who made sure that all the ceremonies were carried out properly. On an island where the sun goes down and stays down for most of the eight months of the winter—and comes up and stays up for most of the four months of summer—and where life itself depends on what can be taken from the sea, people have to make sure that they please the gods.

Because whales are most important to the survival of the Yupik people, there are special songs of petition to the gods before a whale hunt begins, certain rituals to be followed when a whale is captured, and when it is finally beached. Some of the whale must be returned to the ocean, some water from the ocean must be brought to the whale; for like all life, whales have spirits and must be honored. Indeed, Yupiks feel a kinship with the whale, the walrus, and the seal. Do they not all share the same cold waters, fight the same storms, know when the ice comes and when it goes?

Of course some things changed over the years. The islanders, who in the early days lived in caves dug into the hillsides, moved to houses made of walrus skins, and finally to

small wood houses provided by the government. Once, after a famine, the islanders brought reindeer over from Siberia, and reindeer herders started a new town which they called Savoonga. Airplanes came to the island, and an airstrip was built to receive them.

In countries far away there were wars. And finally, in the early 1940s, there was a world war with warships even in their own sea, and with their own men signing up for the National Guard. Yet the Yupiks remained a peaceful people. One thing they thought would never change: Nothing could stop them from visiting back and forth with relatives and friends in Siberia.

Yet there were changes in Siberia too. The day came when Gambell men visiting Siberia found Russians, white men, in the Yupik villages. Some were policemen dressed in uniform who walked about with rifles and billy clubs. The Siberians told their island friends not to worry. When they saw a policeman, they should shout, *"Trastuwu!"* In Russian this is *Zdrasteuite* and is simply a greeting, but to the islanders it sounded like a password. *"Trastuwu,"* they would shout, no matter how far away they were. This seemed to keep them safe, and they visited as they always had.

World War II was over in 1945, but the Siberian Yupiks and the St. Lawrence Yupiks may not have paid much attention to the fact that their two countries were not friendly. Then one day in 1948, the schoolteacher, the only person on St. Lawrence who had a radio, heard some astounding news that had to be passed on quickly to the islanders. The Russian government had passed a law which denied anyone the right to enter Siberia or even Siberian waters. Furthermore, no one from Siberia could leave Siberia.

At first the people on St. Lawrence could not believe such news. How could it be? Had someone forgotten to say the password? Had the teacher heard wrong?

But it was true. The international date line, an imaginary line that runs between Siberia and St. Lawrence, was the point that no one was allowed to cross. Some St. Lawrence men claimed that they could tell where that line was. The water was ruffled at that point, they said, as though currents were crossing each other. And when it was Monday on one side of the line, it was Tuesday on the other side. But from now on they would be stuck in St. Lawrence time and the Siberians would be stuck in Siberian time, with never a word of greeting between them. It was like telling the spring birds not to return next year.

All they could hope for was change, but change did not come. Instead, there were military units in Alaska with their guns ready to turn on Siberia if necessary. And in Siberia, they supposed, it must have been the same. After a while, the is-landers gave up racing and wrestling for basketball. Still, on clear days when they looked across the water to the Siberian hills, they were heartsick.

Ten years passed. Twenty. Thirty. Now only grandparents and the elders remembered what it was like in the old days, but they told the young ones. Then as forty years approached, everyone agreed that this was just too long. Soon even memories would go. What could they do? Some of the islanders had already joined Eskimos from northern Alaska, from Canada, and from Greenland in an Arctic Eskimo organization—the Inuit (Eskimo) Interpolar Conference—to try to persuade the world to make the Arctic a nuclear-free, nonmilitary zone. They knew it might be impossible, but sometimes people had to work for the impossible, didn't they? Still, they needed the Siberian Eskimos to work with them.

Many people in Alaska agreed to help. They wrote letters to the Russian government. They talked to people who talked to other people who in turn talked to people in important places who could say yes or no. Alaskan children wrote notes to Siberian children, attached them to helium balloons, and let them loose over the water, hoping they would float over the international date line into the next day.

Finally the Russian government said yes. One plane load of Eskimos could come for one day to the town of Provideniya on the Siberian coast. It was to be called Friendship Flight One, and surely that meant there would be a Friendship Flight Two and Three, until maybe people could stop counting.

On Tuesday, June 14, 1988, the flight took off. Of course

everyone was excited. Ora Gologergen, a seventy-two-year-old elder from St. Lawrence, hoped to meet a friend she had played with as a girl in Gambell. Darlene Orr, who was in her twenties and too young to have met any Siberians, knew she had relatives somewhere in the area. In Provideniya, not just Eskimos (who made up a small part of the population) were celebrating but the whole town. Russian school children waited for the Friendship Flight, waving American and Russian flags and holding up banners with messages of peace and pictures of doves.

Ora found her childhood friend, but they laughed and cried so much that later she couldn't remember what they had said. Darlene and her aunt, Nancy Walunga, who also went, discovered that their relatives had been relocated to the nearby village of Sirenki and they couldn't go there. Instead, they were invited to tea with a group of local Yupik women. Darlene's aunt had brought tapes of Yupik dances, and when she played these, the women clapped in delight. Although the kitchen where they were sitting was small, the women jumped to their feet, lined up, and danced the old dances together. Then they sat down for a bowl of reindeer meat and a dish of raw fish.

From beginning to end, the day was a success, but best of all, there was a promise of more. Perhaps soon the Siberians could bring a plane of Eskimos to Alaska. Perhaps St. Lawrence islanders could make the trip to Siberia by boat right over the international date line. And yes, perhaps the Siberian Eskimos would be allowed to send representatives to the Interpolar Conference.

For Darlene Orr, the good news was that she would be invited to Sirenki for their annual whale hunt. Later in the summer when she arrived, she found that she was suddenly part of a huge family, all with the same last name. And there they were on a Siberian beach, all of them speaking the same Yupik language as if they had grown up together.

To make everything perfect, the whale hunters got their whale on their first day out. Nothing can bring Yupiks more joy than catching their whale. Not only is it their food for the winter; it is their victory over life in a place where life is hard to live. And when the whale boats came to shore, towing the whale behind them, the crew sang the whale-catch cry together as Yupiks had always done. *"Uu-huk! Uu-huk!"* The very sound of the cry rang with triumph.

Standing on the beach with her new family, watching the traditional ceremony of bringing water to the beached whale and returning part of the whale to the water, Darlene felt lifted beyond herself. She was one with these people, one with all people, one with the land and the sea and the sky which all people shared. At a time like this, one could believe that anything was possible. Not only peace throughout the Arctic, but peace throughout the world.

The Game

by Myra Cohn Livingston

illustrated by Paul O. Zelinsky

Plastic soldiers march on the floor
Off to fight a terrible war.

The green troops charge. The grey side falls.
Guns splatter bullets on the walls.

Tanks move in. Jet fighters zoom
Dropping bombs all over the room.

All the soldiers are dead but two.
The game is over. The war is through.

The plastic soldiers are put away.
What other game is there to play?

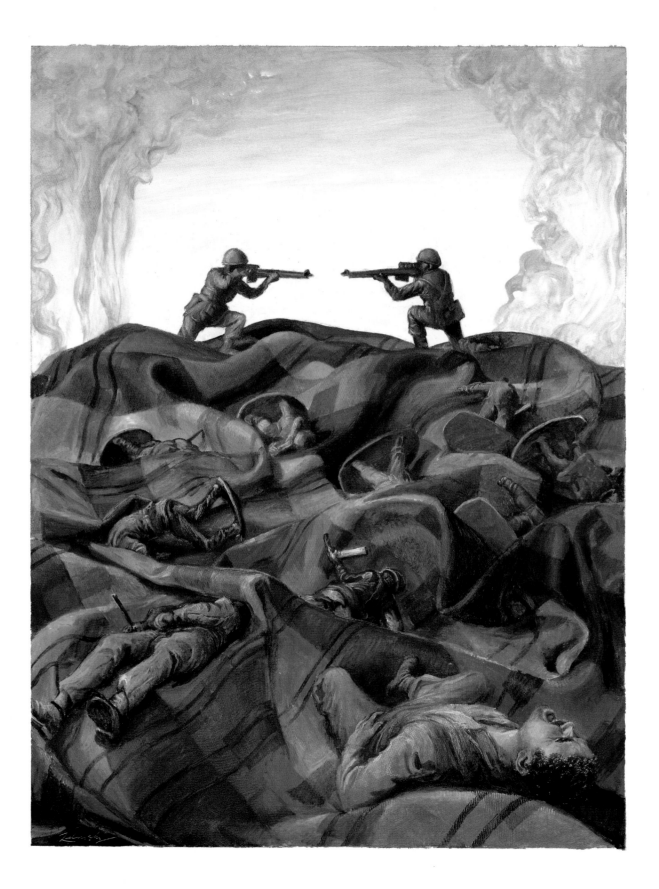

The Tree House

by Lois Lowry

illustrated by Trina Schart Hyman

It was a terrific tree house. *Better* than terrific: It was a marvelous, magnificent, one-of-a-kind tree house, with wooden walls painted bright blue. It had two windows, with red shutters on each, and a yellow door with two shiny brass hinges and a small brass bell that rang when you pulled a string. There was a little porch where you could sit with your legs dangling.

Inside were a table, a chair, a small rug with fringe on each end, and two fat pillows so that you could lie on the rug and read.

You reached it by climbing a ladder—a ladder to the best tree house ever. And it belonged to Chrissy.

"It's all mine, isn't it?" she had asked her grandfather after he built the house for her. "Just mine, and nobody else's?"

Grandpa was washing his paintbrush. He nodded. "I built it just for you," he said.

So Chrissy used her markers and made a sign. CHRISSY'S HOUSE, the sign said. KEEP OUT! She tacked it to the door. Then she took her favorite books into the tree house, curled up on the pillows, and began to read.

"Chrissy?" The voice came from the next yard, from just across the fence.

Chrissy got up and looked through the tree house window. "Hi, Leah," she said to the girl who lived next door. "How do you like my tree house, now that it's all done?"

"It's beautiful," Leah said. "What do you have inside?"

"A table and two chairs and a rug and some pillows," Chrissy told her. "And some secret stuff," she added, though she didn't have secret stuff, really. She *planned* to.

"Can I come up and see?" Leah asked.

"No," Chrissy said. "It's just for me. That's why I made the sign."

Leah stood silently for a moment. Then she said, "I hate you, Chrissy."

"I hate you, too," Chrissy replied. She went back to the pillows and opened her book again.

A short time later, she heard voices in the next yard. She peered through her window and saw that Leah's father was there with Leah. They had a wheelbarrow full of old boards, and a jar of nails. As Chrissy watched from her window, she saw Leah's father prop an old ladder against the trunk of the tree on the other side of the fence. Then, after he jiggled the ladder and made certain it was steady, he climbed up, carrying a board, and began to nail it into place where the branches came together.

He was making Leah a tree house. Chrissy laughed to herself. Leah's father was at home because he had lost his job. She knew they didn't have extra money now for things like paint and brass hinges. And Leah's tree house would never be as good as hers. Never in a million years. Chrissy went back to her book and turned the pages while the hammering continued.

That evening, after supper, Chrissy stood beside the fence and looked up at Leah's finished house. She laughed aloud.

It had taken a week for Grandpa to finish building her beautiful tree house. Grandpa had used new wooden boards from the lumberyard. But Leah's had been completed in a day, and Chrissy could see that it was made from the stack of old weathered boards that had been in the corner of Leah's yard. Only one board remained there now; the others had become the tree house.

The house had walls and a porch and a door and two windows, but it had no shutters and no paint and no door bell. The boards were crooked, and the roof had holes where the pieces of wood didn't quite meet.

Even the sign wasn't as good, because Leah had done hers with crayons instead of marking pens. But its message was the same. Leah's House, it said. Keep Out.

Leah's head appeared in the window of her tree house.

"Your house is not as nice as mine," Chrissy told her.

"Not on the outside," Leah said. "But inside, it's better."

Chrissy wondered what Leah had inside her tree house. But she didn't ask.

For several days the two girls didn't speak to each other. They sat alone in their tree houses. By the fourth day, Chrissy had finished all her books and had read some of them twice. She went to her window and called across the fence to Leah.

"Do you have any books I can borrow?" she asked, when Leah's head appeared.

"No. Our car's broken so we can't go to the library."

"You don't have any books at *all*?"

Leah shook her head.

Chrissy sat back down. She wondered what it would be

like to be in a tree house with no books at all. She wondered what Leah was doing in there.

Finally she called across the fence again. "Would you like to borrow some of mine?" she asked. And Leah said yes.

So Chrissy climbed down, stood at the fence, and handed two books over to Leah, who had climbed down her ladder, too.

"I have some bananas," Leah told her. "Do you want one?" Chrissy nodded, and Leah climbed up and returned with a banana to pass across the fence.

Back in her own tree house, Chrissy peeled and ate the banana. Then she called to Leah again.

"Do you have a wastebasket in your house? I don't want to mess up my carpeting with this banana peel."

Leah, looking through her window, nodded. So Chrissy climbed down, and Leah climbed down, and Chrissy handed the banana peel across the fence.

Both girls climbed back into their houses. Chrissy sat alone and admired her fringed rug for a moment, then leafed through her books again, wondering what Leah was doing. She called through her window.

"Leah?"

Leah looked out. "What?"

"I could come visit you if you want," Chrissy said.

Leah didn't answer.

"Or you could come visit me," Chrissy added.

"Your sign says KEEP OUT," Leah pointed out. "So does mine."

"Well," Chrissy suggested, "we could change them."

Leah nodded. Each girl removed her sign and crossed out the words KEEP OUT. They wrote WELCOME instead. They rehung their signs.

"You know what, Chrissy?" Leah said. "We could use that wide board in the corner of my yard. It would go from your porch to my porch, over the top of the fence. Then we could visit each other by walking across the board."

Chrissy eyed the distance and the height. "What if we fell?"

"It's not very high," Leah pointed out. "And if we each came out halfway and held hands, we could help each other across."

They climbed down their ladders. The wide board was heavy, but when each girl took an end they were able to lift it into place. In a few minutes they had made a bridge between the houses, over the top of the fence.

Chrissy stepped from her tree house porch onto the wide board, reached for Leah's waiting hand, and walked across. She entered Leah's tree house and looked around.

There was no rug, and the only books were her own that Leah had borrowed. But there was a bowl of fruit, a wastebasket, and curtains at the windows. The walls were covered with portraits of beautiful women—the most beautiful women Chrissy had ever seen.

"I like your art collection, Leah," Chrissy said.

"They're left over from where my mom works," Leah explained. "She works at a beauty parlor, and they get pictures of all the new hairstyles. These are last year's."

"You can't tell. They look brand new."

"My house isn't as nice as yours," Leah added. "I said it was better inside, but it isn't, really."

"I don't really have carpeting," Chrissy admitted. "Only an old rug. And I don't have curtains, or a single picture on my walls."

"I could let you have one of my pictures. Two, even. You can have the blonde shag and the auburn blunt cut."

"My grandpa had paint left over. He could paint the outside of your house so we'd match. But I'm afraid we don't have another door bell."

"Now that my sign says WELCOME, I don't think I need a door bell," Leah said.

"I don't really hate you, Leah," Chrissy said.

"I don't really hate you, either," Leah replied.

They sat together on Leah's porch and looked around happily.

"What do you think is the best part of a tree house, Chrissy?" Leah asked.

Chrissy thought. She looked over at her own house, with its shutters and brass hinges. She looked around at Leah's, with its bowl of bright apples and its yellow curtains.

"The *very* best part," she said finally, "is the bridge."

They That Take the Sword

A TRUE STORY

by Milton Meltzer

illustrated by Leonard Everett Fisher

Who has ever heard of Seth Laughlin?

I hadn't until one day I saw that name in print in a book. I like to play with names, to see where they come from and what they mean. *Laugh-lin*—say it that way and it sounds funny. I read on to see if his story was laughable.

Not quite.

Seth lived in the South, in Virginia. It was in the time before the Civil War, when most black people in the South were slaves. Seth's family was not well-off. They owned no slaves. As Seth grew up, he began to think that slavery was wrong. How can one person feel it is all right for him to own another person? To deny him his freedom to live his own life?

But he found no other white people in his village who thought the way he did. Seth married, and over the years had seven children. Together they made a living on their small farm. Early on, Seth stopped going to church. The preacher said nothing about the evil of slavery. Sometimes he even praised it. Christians, he said, were doing God's will when they took black people under their wing and protected them, giving them work to do and a place to live, and food to eat, and clothing to wear. (And paying them nothing, and buying and selling them like cattle, and not letting them learn to read, and whipping them when they liked, and a thousand other sins against human decency, Seth thought.)

It made Seth sick to sit there and listen to the preacher. One day he heard there were some people in the town nearby who thought the way he did. They were called Quakers, and they held weekly meetings. He saddled his horse and rode over on a Sunday morning. He liked what they said in their meeting. It made him feel stronger to know others thought as he did.

But he found the Quakers were not only against slavery,

they were against war, too. They lived by what Jesus said in his Sermon on the Mount: "Blessed are the peacemakers: for they shall be called the children of God." And Jesus had told Peter, "All they that take the sword shall perish with the sword."

What did that mean? That violence does no good in the long run? That to meet violence with violence is only to create a cycle of violence that never ends?

Now some Quakers did not believe it was enough to detest slavery and war. To be against using violence does not mean you give in quietly to injustice. You oppose it with all the moral strength you have. And take the consequences. Even when it means defying the right of government to order you to carry out its law when that law goes against your conscience.

Soon after Seth joined the Quakers, Abraham Lincoln was elected president of the United States. With his victory, the South knew the federal government would not allow slavery to be spread into the new territories of the West. Southern states broke away from the Union and began the Civil War by firing on the federal garrison at Fort Sumter.

On both sides, the South and the North, men volunteered to fight or were drafted into the armies. What should I do now, Seth wondered. Some of the Quakers he knew fled North to avoid the draft. Others hid in forests or caves. But Seth stayed at home with his family. The war went on, year after year, with tens of thousands of men killed on both sides, and the land ruined wherever the fighting raged. Now the South began to draft both young boys and older men, to fill the empty ranks.

One day—it was 1863—an Army officer came to get Seth. He refused to go.

"It is against my conscience to shed blood," he said, "no matter what the cause."

"Then pay the fee of five hundred dollars," the officer said, "and we will get someone to take your place."

"No," said Seth. "I am glad not to take up arms to protect slavery. And I will not pay to have another man do it in my place."

So the officer arrested Seth, handcuffed him, and took him to an army camp near Petersburg.

"We will break this man's spirit," said the colonel, "and he will be glad to do as we ask."

A sergeant took Seth away and ordered him to stand, without any support, for thirty-six hours. A soldier stood nearby, and every time sleepiness overcame Seth and he began to sag to his knees, the soldier pierced him with a bayonet to make him stand straight again.

"Are you ready to obey orders now?" the sergeant asked.

Seth shook his head.

"Then buck him down," said the sergeant.

The soldiers threw him to the ground, tied his wrists together, slipping them over his knees, and then ran a stick

through the space between his knees and over his arms. They kept him in this painful position for three hours a day, day after day.

A week later: "Are you ready to join up now?"

"No," said Seth.

"Then tie him up," said the sergeant.

They suspended Seth by the thumbs from the branch of a tree so that his toes barely touched the ground. He was left in that position for an hour and a half, each day, for a week. The pain was agonizing.

Thinking Seth was conquered, the sergeant cut him down and handed him a rifle. Seth dropped it on the ground. Then they gagged him by forcing a thick piece of wood into his mouth and tying it tight. The strain on his teeth and jaws was unbearable. Still he did not give in. More threats, more devices to torture him. Still no surrender. In desperate anger, the colonel ordered him court-martialed.

A military court sat to hear the evidence against Seth. Then it convicted him of refusal to obey orders, and commanded him to be shot.

The troops were paraded onto the execution ground, to learn a lesson. Twelve privates were detailed to carry out the death sentence. Six guns were loaded with bullets, six with blank cartridges, and they were handed to the twelve chosen men.

Seth, as calm as any of the men surrounding him, asked

for time to pray. Of course they could not deny him this. The colonel assumed that naturally Seth would pray for himself.

But Seth was ready to meet his Lord. And so he prayed not for himself, but for them: "Father, forgive them, for they know not what they do."

As the soldiers heard his firm voice and the meaning of his words sank in, each of the twelve men lowered his gun. Accustomed as they were to taking human life, and knowing the penalty for disobeying military orders, they resolutely declared they could not shoot such a man. But the chosen twelve were not the only ones whose hearts were touched. The officers of the military court themselves revoked the sentence. Seth was sent instead to prison.

There he fell sick from the heavy punishment he had undergone. And after a long illness, he passed quietly away.

Law of the Great Peace

*adapted by John Bierhorst from
the Iroquois Book of the Great Law*

illustrated by Barbara Cooney

1

With the statesmen of the League of
Five Nations, I plant the Tree of
Great Peace.

2

I name the tree the Tree of the
Great Long Leaves.

3

Under the shade of this Tree of
Great Peace, we spread the soft,
white, feathery down of the globe
thistle as seats for you.

4

Roots have spread out from the Tree
of Great Peace, one to the north,
one to the east, one to the south,
and one to the west. These are the
Great White Roots, and their nature
is peace and strength.

5

The smoke of the council fire of
the League shall ascend and pierce
the sky so that other nations who
may be allies may see the council
fire of the Great Peace.

6

You, the League of Five Nations
chiefs, be firm so that if a tree

should fall upon your joined hands,
it shall not separate you or weaken
your hold. So shall the strength
of union be preserved.

7

The Great Creator has made us of
one blood, and of the same soil.

8

When a member of an alien nation
comes to the territory of the
League and seeks refuge and
permanent residence, the statesmen
of the nation to which he comes
shall extend hospitality and make
him a member of the nation.

9

Whenever a foreign nation enters
the League or accepts the Great
Peace, the Five Nations and the
foreign nation shall enter into an
agreement by which the foreign

nation shall try to persuade the other
nations to accept the Great Peace.

10

I now uproot the tallest tree, and
into the hole thereby made, we cast
all weapons of war. Into the
depths of the earth, down into the
deep underneath currents of water
flowing to unknown regions, we cast
all the weapons of strife. We bury
them from sight and we plant again
the tree. Thus shall the Great
Peace be established, and
hostilities shall no longer be
known between the Five Nations, but
peace to the united people.

Note: Well before the English settlements at Jamestown and Plymouth, the five Iroquois tribes of the region that would someday become New York joined in a "great peace." Other tribes, or nations, were invited to seek shelter within the league, and several, including the Tuscarora, an Iroquoian tribe of North Carolina, eventually did so.

Today the original five nations—Mohawk, Oneida, Onondaga, Cayuga, and Seneca—together with the Tuscarora, still observe the Law of the Great Peace and honor the memory of the league's founder, Deganawida, who planted the "tree" and spread the soft "thistle down" where the first peacemakers held their councils.

(Sources: Arthur C. Parker, *The Constitution of the Five Nations,* New York State Museum Bulletin 184, 1916; John Fadden, *Kaianerekowa Hotinonsionne,* Mohawk Nation at Akwesasne, 1971.)

The Bus for Deadhorse

by Natalie Babbitt

illustrated by Jon Agee

There was a nice old man once—his name was Mr. Moon—who was rich as a king and lived in a big house full of beautiful things. He had four children, but they weren't nice at all. They had grown up greedy and quarrelsome, as different from the old man as they could be. Those four could start an argument over anything, even whether rain was wet. They were so disagreeable that Mr. Moon gave up on them, finally, and turned his attention to his cat.

Then one day the old man came down with a fever and took to his bed, where he stayed for days and days. The doctors tried everything they could think of but nothing seemed to help, and at last they called the children together and told them it was likely that Mr. Moon wouldn't last much longer.

So the children—except, remember, they were all grown up—hung about in their father's house, waiting for the end. And while they hung about, they looked at all the beautiful things.

"When the time comes," said one, "I get the silver bowl."

"No, *I* want the bowl," said the second. "I always liked it best. You can have the forks and spoons."

"Those forks and spoons were meant for *me,*" said the third. "You can have the breakfast china and the paintings. A few of the paintings, anyway, because I want most of them."

"Well, I want some paintings, too, and the breakfast china and the big lace tablecloth," said the fourth. "So you'll have to be satisfied with the mantel clock. And I'm taking the suit of armor from the upstairs hall."

"Oh, no, you aren't," said the first. "That's mine."

"What makes you think you ought to get the silver bowl *and* the armor?" said the fourth.

"The same thing that makes you think you're going to get

the tablecloth, the breakfast china, and the paintings," said the first.

They argued and argued, getting noisier all the time, until at last the doctors came downstairs and said, "This racket you're making is disgraceful with your father so sick. You'll have to leave the house if you can't keep quiet."

Well, of course the children—except, don't forget they were all grown up—couldn't keep quiet for a minute, so they had to leave the house. And at the corner they were still so busy arguing that they got on the wrong bus: It wasn't the crosstown bus at all, but a special bus headed for Deadhorse, Alaska, which is so far north that there's nothing to do there but shiver, and the children didn't even notice until it was too late to get off. So there they were in Deadhorse, where the bus froze over and couldn't come back, and the children were never heard from again.

In the meantime, old Mr. Moon suddenly took a turn for the better, much to the joy of his cat—and his doctors—and in a day or two he was up and about, good as new. He did wonder for a while what had become of his children. But in case it slipped your mind, they were all grown up after all, and able to take care of themselves, so Mr. Moon didn't worry much about them. After a few years he simply changed his will, leaving the house and all his beautiful things to be turned into a

Home for Wandering Cats, with his own cat to have the best front bedroom.

And this is the way it all worked out. Cats came from far and wide when the Home was opened, and lived long, happy lives there. They took turns napping in the silver bowl and ate their tuna and liver from the breakfast china in perfect harmony. And they never ever took the wrong bus. In fact, there never was another bus for Deadhorse, Alaska, after the first one. And isn't that peculiar!

Letter from a Concentration Camp

by Yoshiko Uchida

illustrated by Allen Say

Mailing Address: Barrack 16, Apartment 40
Tanforan Assembly Center
San Bruno, California

Actual Address: Stable 16, Horse stall 40
Tanforan Racetrack

May 6, 1942

Dear Hermie:

Here I am sitting on an army cot in a smelly old horse stall, where Mama, Bud, and I have to live for who knows how long. It's pouring rain, the wind's blowing in through all the cracks, and Mama looks like she wants to cry. I guess she misses Papa. Or maybe what got her down was that long, muddy walk along the racetrack to get to the mess hall for supper.

Anyway, now I know how it feels to stand in line at a soup kitchen with hundreds of hungry people. And that cold potato and weiner they gave me sure didn't make me feel much better. I'm still hungry, and I'd give you my last nickel if you appeared this minute with a big fat hamburger and a bagful of cookies.

You know what? It's like being in jail here—not being free to live in your own house, do what you want, or eat what you want. They've got barbed wire all around this racetrack and guard towers at each corner to make sure we can't get out. Doesn't that sound like a prison? It sure feels like one!

What I want to know is, What am I doing here anyway? *Me*—a genuine born-in-California citizen of the United States of America stuck behind barbed wire, just because I *look* like the enemy in Japan. And how come you're not in here too, with that German blood in your veins and a name like Herman Schnabel. We're at war with Germany too, aren't we? And with Italy? What about the people at Napoli Grocers?

My brother, Bud, says the US government made a terrible mistake that they'll regret someday. He says our leaders betrayed us and ignored the Constitution. But you know what I think? I think war makes people crazy. Why else would a smart man like President Franklin D. Roosevelt sign an executive order to

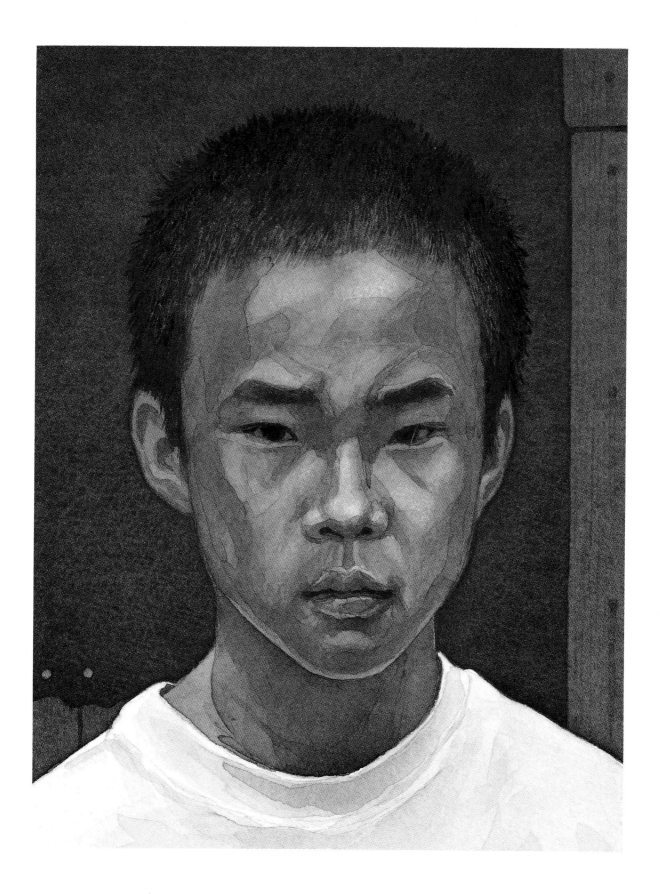

force us Japanese Americans out of our homes and lock us up in concentration camps? Why else would the FBI take Papa off to a POW camp just because he worked for a Japanese company? Papa—who loves America just as much as they do.

Hey, ask Mrs. Wilford what that was all about. I mean that stuff she taught us in sixth grade about the Bill of Rights and due process of law. If that means everybody can have a hearing before being thrown in prison, how come nobody gave us a hearing? I guess President Roosevelt forgot about the Constitution when he ordered us into concentration camps. I told you war makes people crazy!

Well, Hermie, I gotta go now. Mama says we should get to the showers before the hot water runs out like it did when she went to do the laundry. Tomorrow she's getting up at 4:00 A.M. to beat the crowd. Can you imagine having to get up in the middle of the night and stand in line to wash your sheets and towels? By hand too! No luxuries like washing machines in this dump!

Hey, do me a favor? Go pet my dog, Rascal, for me. He's probably wondering why I had to leave him with Mrs. Harper next door. Tell him I'll be back to get him for sure. It's just that I don't know when. There's a rumor we're getting shipped to some desert—probably in Utah. But don't worry, when this stupid war is over, I'm coming home to California and nobody's ever going to kick me out again! You just wait and see! So long, Hermie.

Your pal,
Jimbo Kurasaki

Note: In 1942, shortly after the outbreak of war with Japan, the United States government uprooted and imprisoned, without trial or hearing, 120,000 Americans of Japanese ancestry. They were sent first to "assembly centers" located in abandoned racetracks and fairgrounds. From there they were sent to ten bleak concentration camps located in remote areas of the country.

In 1976 President Gerald R. Ford stated, "not only was that evacuation wrong, but Japanese Americans were and are loyal Americans." In 1983 a commission established by the Congress of the United States concluded that a grave injustice had been done to Americans of Japanese descent. It also stated that the causes of the uprooting were race prejudice, war hysteria, and a failure of political leadership.

Enemies

by Charlotte Zolotow

illustrated by Ben Shecter

We watch
        TV

and see
        enemies fighting.

Close-ups of
        narrow faces
        deep dark eyes
        full young lips.

There are
        two.
Which is an Arab?
        Which a Jew?

The Birds' Peace

by Jean Craighead George

illustrated by Ted Rand

On the day Kristy's father went off to war, she burst out
the back door and ran down the path to the woods. Her eyes
hurt. Her chest burned. She crossed the bridge over the purling
stream and dashed into the lean-to she and her father had built
near the edge of the flower-filled woodland meadow.

She dropped to her knees, then to her belly. Covering her face with both hands, she sobbed from the deepest well of her being.

Tears did not help. The pain went on and on.

A bird sang.

Kristy lifted her head. She recognized Fluter, the busy little song sparrow who lived in the bushes at the edge of the meadow. He seemed to be in trouble. His melodious song was loud and belligerent.

"I'm in trouble, too," she said. "My father had to go into the army. He's going to war. And I am scared." Fluter ignored her and sang on. From across the meadow, a strange song sparrow sang clearly and loudly. Kristy barely heard him.

"Daddy doesn't even know how to shoot a gun."

Fluter flew to a sumac bush, thrust out his spotted tan breast, and sang again.

"Suppose bombs fall on him." Kristy began to cry again. "Or an enemy tank shoots at him."

Fluter went on singing. After a few moments he flew across the meadow and boldly sang from a raspberry patch.

Dulce, his mate, flew off their nest in the thicket, where she had been incubating their eggs. She ate a bristlegrass seed and serenely preened her feathers. She was quite at ease.

Fluter was not. He turned this way and that. He flicked his tail and raised his crest, then flew to the bracken fern and sang. He flitted briskly to the sugar maple limb and sang from a conspicuous twig. He winged to the dogwood tree and sang from a high limb. As he flew and sang, Kristy became aware of what he was doing. He was making a circle, an invisible fence of song around his meadow and his nest in the thicket.

Suddenly Fluter clicked out what Kristy's father had told her were notes of warning. Dulce became alarmed. She flattened her feathers to her body and flew silently back to their nest.

Kristy checked to see what was the matter. The strange song sparrow was in Fluter's raspberry bush. He was pointing his bill at Fluter, who crouched as if he were going to fly at the stranger. But he did not. Instead, he sang.

The stranger heard Fluter's "stay-off-my-property" song and swiftly departed. He flew over Fluter's invisible fence of song and alighted on his own sapling. There he sang at Fluter.

Fluter flew to the sugar maple limb on the border of his territory and sang right back at him. The stranger answered with a flood of melody from his trees and bushes. When each understood where the other's territory lay, they rested and preened their feathers.

Kristy was fascinated. She sat up and crossed her legs.

"Even Daddy doesn't know about this," she said.

Putting her chin in her hands, she watched the birds until the day's long shadows told her she must go home. And all that time, Fluter did not fly or sing beyond the raspberry bush, nor did the stranger come back to Fluter's territory. But sing they did, brightly and melodically, while their mates sat serenely on their brown-splotched eggs.

Dear Daddy, Kristy wrote that night. *I know how the birds keep the peace.*

The Silent Lobby

by Mildred Pitts Walter

illustrated by Jerry Pinkney

The old bus chugged along the Mississippi highway toward Washington, D.C. I shivered from icy winds and from excitement and fear. Excitement about going to Washington and fear that the old bus would stall again on the dark, lonely, icy road and we'd never make it.

Oh, just to sleep. The chug-chug-chugging of the old motor was not smooth enough to make soothing sounds, and I could not forget the words Mama and Papa had said just before me and Papa left to pick up twenty other people who filled the bus.

"It's too dangerous," Mama had said. "They just might bomb that bus."

"They could bomb this house for that matter," Papa said.

"I know," Mama went on. "That's why I don't want you to go. Why can't you just forget about this voting business and let us live in peace?"

"There can be no peace without freedom," Papa said.

"And you think someone is going to give you freedom?" Mama asked with heat in her voice. "Instead of going to Washington, you should be getting a gun to protect us."

"There are ways to win a struggle without bombs and guns. I'm going to Washington and Craig is going with me."

"Craig is too young."

"He's eleven. That's old enough to know what this is all about," Papa insisted.

I knew. It had all started two years ago, in 1963. Papa was getting ready to go into town to register to vote. Just as he was leaving, Mr. Clem, Papa's boss, came and warned Papa that he should not try to register.

"I intend to register," Papa said.

"If you do, I'll have to fire you." Mr. Clem drove away in a cloud of dust.

"You ought not go," Mama said, alarmed. "You know that people have been arrested and beaten for going down there."

"I'm going," Papa insisted.

"Let me go with you, Papa." I was scared, too, and wanted to be with him if he needed help.

"No, you stay and look after your mama and the house till I get back."

Day turned to night, and Papa had not returned. Mama paced the floor. Was Papa in jail? Had he been beaten. We waited, afraid. Finally, I said, "Mama, I'll go find him."

"Oh, no!" she cried. Her fear scared me more, and I felt angry because I couldn't do anything.

At last we heard Papa's footsteps. The look on his face let us know right away that something was mighty wrong.

"What happened, Sylvester?" Mama asked.

"I paid the poll tax, passed the literacy test, but I didn't interpret the state constitution the way they wanted. So they wouldn't register me."

Feeling a sense of sad relief, I said, "Now you won't lose your job."

"Oh, but I will. I tried to register."

Even losing his job didn't stop Papa from wanting to vote.

One day he heard about Mrs. Fannie Lou Hamer and the Mississippi Freedom Democratic Party. The Freedom Party registered people without charging a poll tax, without a literacy test, and without people having to tell what the Mississippi Constitution was about.

On election day in 1964, Papa proudly voted for Mrs. Hamer, Mrs. Victoria Grey, and Mrs. Annie Devine to represent the people of the Second Congressional District of Mississippi. Eighty-three thousand other black men and women voted that day, too. Great victory celebrations were held in homes and churches. But the Governor of Mississippi, Paul B. Johnson, declared all of those eighty-three thousand votes of black people illegal. He gave certificates of election to three white men—William Colmer, John Williams, and a Mr. Whittier—to represent the mostly black Second Congressional District.

Members of the Freedom Party were like Papa—they didn't give up. They got busy when the governor threw out their votes. Lawyers from all over the country came to help. People signed affidavits saying that when they tried to register they lost their jobs, they were beaten, and their homes were burned and churches bombed. More than ten thousand people signed petitions to the governor asking him to count their votes. There was never a word from the governor.

My mind returned to the sound of the old bus slowly grinding along. Suddenly the bus stopped. Not again! We'd never make it now. Papa got out in the cold wind and icy drizzling rain and raised the hood. While he worked, we sang and clapped our hands to keep warm. I could hear Sister Phyllis praying with all her might for our safety. After a while we were moving along again.

I must have finally fallen asleep, for a policeman's voice woke me. "You can't stop here near the Capitol," he shouted.

"Our bus won't go," Papa said.

"If you made it from Mississippi all the way to D.C., you'll make it from here," the policeman barked.

At first the loud voice frightened me. Then, wide awake, sensing the policeman's impatience, I wondered why Papa didn't let him know that we would go as soon as the motor started. But Papa, knowing that old bus, said nothing. He stepped on the starter. The old motor growled and died. Again the policeman shouted, "I said get out of here."

"We'll have to push it," Papa said.

Everyone got off the bus and pushed. Passersby stopped and stared. Finally we were safe on a side street, away from the Capitol with a crowd gathered around us.

"You mean they came all the way from Mississippi in that?" someone in the crowd asked.

Suddenly the old bus looked shabby. I lowered my head

and became aware of my clothes: my faded coat too small; my cotton pants too thin. With a feeling of shame, I wished those people would go away.

"What brings you all to the District?" a man called to us.

"We've come to see about seating the people we voted for and elected," Papa answered. "Down home they say our votes don't count, and up here they've gone ahead and seated men who don't represent us. We've come to talk about that."

"So you've come to lobby," a woman shouted. The crowd laughed.

Why were they laughing? I knew that to lobby meant to try to get someone to decide for or against something. Yes, that was why we had come. I wished I could have said to those people who stood gawking at us that the suffering that brought us here was surely nothing to laugh about.

The laughter from the crowd quieted when another woman shouted, "You're too late to lobby. The House of Representatives will vote on that issue this morning."

Too late. That's what had worried me when the old bus kept breaking down. Had we come so far in this cold for nothing? Was it really too late to talk to members of the House of Representatives to persuade them to seat our representatives elected by the Freedom Party, *not* the ones chosen by the governor?

Just then rain began to fall. The crowd quickly left, and

we climbed onto our bus. Papa and the others started to talk. What would we do now? Finally, Papa said, "We can't turn back now. We've done too much and come too far."

After more talk we all agreed that we must try to do what we had come to do. Icy rain pelted us as we rushed against cold wind back to the Capitol.

A doorman stopped us on the steps. "May I have your passes?"

"We don't have any," Papa replied.

"Sorry, you have to have passes for seats in the gallery." The doorman blocked the way.

"We're cold in this rain. Let us in," Sister Phyllis cried.

"Maybe we should just go on back home," someone suggested.

"Yes. We can't talk to the legislators now, anyway," another woman said impatiently.

"No," Papa said. "We must stay if we do no more than let them see that we have come all this way."

"But we're getting soaking wet. We can't stand out here much longer," another protested.

"Can't you just let us in out of this cold?" Papa pleaded with the doorman.

"Not without passes." The doorman still blocked the way. Then he said, "There's a tunnel underneath this building. You can go there to get out of the rain."

We crowded into the tunnel and lined up along the sides. My chilled body and hands came to life pressed against the warm walls. Then footsteps and voices echoed through the tunnel. Police. This tunnel . . . a trap! Would they do something to us for trying to get in without passes? I wanted to cry out to Papa, but I could not speak.

The footsteps came closer. Then many people began to walk by. When they came upon us, they suddenly stopped talking. Only the sound of their feet echoed in the tunnel. Where had they come from? What did they do? "Who are they, Papa?" I whispered.

"Congressmen and women." Papa spoke so softly, I hardly heard him, even in the silence.

They wore warm coats, some trimmed with fur. Their shoes gleamed. Some of them frowned at us. Others glared. Some sighed quickly as they walked by. Others looked at us, then turned their eyes to their shoes. I could tell by a sudden lift of the head and a certain look that some were surprised and scared. And there were a few whose friendly smiles seemed to say, Right on!

I glanced at Papa. How poor he and our friends looked beside those well-dressed people. Their clothes were damp, threadbare, and wrinkled; their shoes were worn and mud stained. But they all stood straight and tall.

My heart pounded. I wanted to call out to those men and

women, "Count my papa's vote! Let my people help make laws, too." But I didn't dare speak in that silence.

Could they hear my heart beating? Did they know what was on my mind? "Lord," I prayed, "let them hear us in this silence."

Then two congressmen stopped in front of Papa. I was frightened until I saw smiles on their faces.

"I'm Congressman Ryan from New York," one of them said. Then he introduced a black man: "This is Congressman Hawkins from California."

"I'm Sylvester Saunders. We are here from Mississippi," Papa said.

"We expected you much earlier," Congressman Ryan said.

"Our old bus and bad weather delayed us," Papa explained.

"That's unfortunate. You could've helped us a lot. We worked late into the night lobbying to get votes on your side. But maybe I should say on *our* side." Mr. Ryan smiled.

"And we didn't do very well," Congressman Hawkins said.

"We'll be lucky if we get fifty votes on our side today," Congressman Ryan informed us. "Maybe you would like to come in and see us at work."

"We don't have passes," I said, surprised at my voice.

"We'll see about getting all of you in," Congressman Hawkins promised.

A little later, as we found seats in the gallery, Congressman Gerald Ford from the state of Michigan was speaking. He did not want Mrs. Hamer and other fairly elected members of the Freedom Party seated in the House. He asked his fellow congressmen to stick to the rule of letting only those with credentials from their states be seated in Congress. The new civil rights act would, in time, undo wrongs done to black Americans. But for now, Congress should let the men chosen by Governor Johnson keep their seats and get on with other business.

Then Congressman Ryan rose to speak. How could Congress stick to rules that denied blacks their right to vote in the state of Mississippi? The rule of letting only those with credentials from a segregated state have seats in the House could not *justly* apply here.

I looked down on those men and few women and wondered if they were listening. Did they know about the petitions? I remembered what Congressman Ryan had said: "We'll be lucky if we get fifty. . . ." Only 50 out of 435 elected to the House.

Finally the time came for Congress to vote. Those who wanted to seat Mrs. Hamer and members of the Freedom Democratic Party were to say, yes. Those who didn't want to seat Mrs. Hamer were to say, no.

At every yes vote I could hardly keep from clapping my

hands and shouting, "Yea! Yea!" But I kept quiet, counting: thirty, then forty, forty-eight . . . only two more. We would lose badly.

Then something strange happened. Congressmen and congresswomen kept saying "Yes. Yes. Yes." On and on, "Yes." My heart pounded. Could we win? I sat on my hands to keep from clapping. I looked at Papa and the others who had come with us. They all sat on the edge of their seats. They looked as if they could hardly keep from shouting out, too, as more yes votes rang from the floor.

When the voting was over, 148 votes had been cast in our favor. What had happened? Why had so many changed their minds?

Later, Papa introduced me to Congressman Hawkins. The congressman asked me, "How did you all know that some of us walk through that tunnel from our offices?"

"We didn't know," I answered. "We were sent there out of the rain."

"That's strange," the congressman said. "Your standing there silently made a difference in the vote. Even though we lost this time, some of them now know that we'll keep on lobbying until we win."

I felt proud. Papa had been right when he said to Mama, "There are ways to win a struggle without bombs and guns." We had lobbied in silence and we had been *heard*.

Note : This story is a fictional account of one demonstration by African Americans during the decade of the 1960s. Many nonviolent demonstrations were held for voting rights, for jobs, and for freedom to use restaurants, libraries, schools, and public restrooms. This one took place on January 4, 1965.

On June 29, 1964, President Lyndon Baines Johnson signed the Omnibus Civil Rights Act banning discrimination in voting, jobs, public facilities, and in housing. On August 6, 1965, President Johnson signed the Voting Rights Act, which guarantees the right to vote without penalties or poll taxes.

A Wild Safe Place

by Maurice Sendak

One More Time

illustrated by
Diane and Leo Dillon

words and music by
Nancy Willard

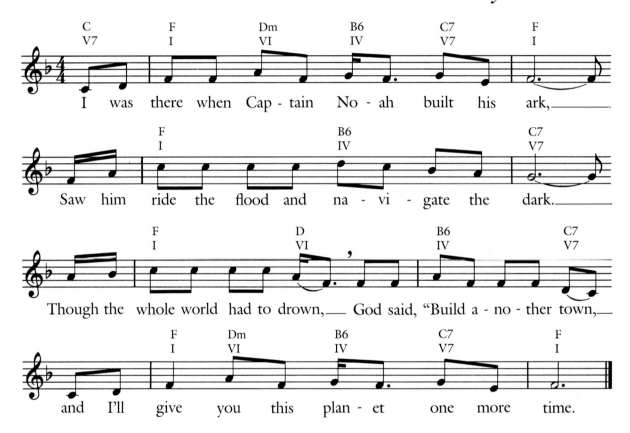

I was there when they took my Lord away,
And I saw Him raise His hand and heard Him say,
"Little children, don't you cry.
Though I'm hung and left to die,
We will break bread together one more time."

I was there when they dropped the atom bomb.
In a flash all our homes and schools were gone.
When we've cleared away the dead,
Give me stones and give me bread.
We will build up our cities one more time.

Someone passing through this forest made a fire,
Let it go till it burned through bush and briar.
Though it's not for you or me,
I am going to plant a tree,
And the forest will grow here one more time.

Dreamed that Death came to carry me away.
Dreamed I saw him drag his feet and heard him say,
"Though I'm skull and bones to you,
I was young and happy too.
Let me stand in the sunlight one more time."

I Was There

by Marilyn Sachs

illustrated by Marc Simont

When they tried to take down the big trees in the park,
I WAS THERE.

I sat in my stroller and ate a pretzel.

The trees stayed up.

When the public library gave a big party to raise money
for a new building,
                    I WAS THERE.

My brother read me a story about a little bear.

They're building a new library right now.

When Charles T. Morrison ran for mayor,
some people worked down at his campaign
headquarters to help get him elected.

I stuffed envelopes.

He didn't get elected.

Maybe he will next time.

When a war broke out, some people marched in a
parade to protest.

I WAS THERE.

I carried a banner that said War Isn't Good For Children.

The war didn't stop. So then there was another parade.

And another.

And many, many others.

I was at some of them.
Sometimes I carried a banner. Sometimes I sang songs.
And sometimes I ate sandwiches.

After a while, the war ended, and we had a picnic in the park to celebrate.

AND

I WAS THERE

A Midnight Clear

by Katherine Paterson

illustrated by Thomas B. Allen

In the middle of the algebra test, Jeff saw the cloud for the first time. He couldn't make heads or tails of the fifth problem, so he did as he usually did when he was stuck: He looked out of the window. That was when he saw it—a huge mushroom cloud with an orange belly, oozing up from the new row houses across from the high school. He threw his hand in front of his eyes. His pencil bounced off the desk and clattered onto the floor.

"Pitman?" Mr. Channing asked. "You all right, Pitman?"

The cloud had disappeared. Behind the row houses there was nothing but a blue December sky. Jeff shook his head at the algebra teacher and leaned down for his pencil. The algebra test was a blur of blue lines and smudges. He picked the pencil up, gathered his books and notebooks from under the seat, and stumbled to the front of the room.

"You sick, Pitman?"

"Yeah, I think so. Like I'm gonna throw up or something." He didn't bother to ask Channing to let him finish the test later. He just handed it over and walked out of the school, back to the apartment. His mother would be furious. No, not furious. Before the divorce she got furious; now she got hurt or hysterical. He preferred furious, but then nobody was asking him.

He took a glass of milk out of the refrigerator. The mail had come. He picked up *Newsweek* to read while he drank his milk. There was a picture of a mushroom cloud on the cover. His skin prickled all over, and he dropped the magazine to the floor. Not the milk. He was lucky it wasn't the milk.

At least that was a real picture of an atomic blast, not a hallucination. Because during the next few days, he saw, or thought he saw, the orange-bellied cloud three more times—once in English class and twice in nightmares.

Then school was out for the holidays. And one day Jeff went downtown, determined to do his shopping, although he didn't even want to think about Christmas. It brought back too many memories—like the time when he was about three and his father took him to see the department store's Santa Claus.

Just as Jeff had gotten to the head of the line, the bearded guy had looked him straight in the eye and boomed out, "Ho! Ho! Ho!" Jeff had screamed for his daddy, and his daddy had come running and picked him up. And his dad hadn't been embarrassed or anything. In fact, he'd fussed at the Santa for laughing so loud and scaring little kids. Jeff still remembered how his father had carried him all the way home.

"That wasn't the real Santa Claus," he had told Jeff. "Just a make-believe. A fake. Didn't even know how to laugh." And they'd both giggled at how stupid the old guy had been. . . . It had been a long time since the two of them had giggled together.

Jeff was going up the escalator, half-listening to the rinky-dink carols being played on the department store's loud-speaker—they were fake as that old Santa's laugh had been—when he saw the mushroom cloud again, right inside the department store, against the wall above the men's sweaters.

"Watch out! What do you think you're doing?" But Jeff ignored the protests, pushing his way down the up escalator as fast as he could and out the front door of the store.

He was breathing hard and sweating despite the cold. "Peace on the earth . . ." God, what a laugh. He was almost crying.

He began walking out rapidly from the center of town. How long before it will all be gone? he wondered. Exploding in the sky or smothered in freezing darkness—either way it would all be gone. A stray dog watched him coming and waited until Jeff drew alongside, lifting its nose and staring with sad brown eyes into Jeff's face.

He knows, Jeff thought. Just a dumb mutt, and he knows.

There were red-colored and tinsel ropes strung between the light posts and on each post a plastic candle in dirty yellow.

What man would destroy, he first makes rinky-dink. Jeff kicked a beer bottle someone had thrown down. It skimmied across the pavement and crashed against concrete steps.

"Hey, watch it!" The screech came from an old woman who was sitting on the steps. "Ain't you got no respect?"

"I'm sorry." Jeff began to pick up the shattered brown glass.

"God's gonna get you, sonny." She jerked her head towards the building behind her. It was a large, greying stucco church. "God's gonna get you good."

"I really am sorry."

She must have been wearing four or five layers of clothes, and her head was wrapped in rags. He could even see the dingy lace of an ancient slip hanging out from under the tatters. Beside her on the steps were two large shopping bags. She reached into one of them and dug around, finally bringing out a large blue kerchief. She blew her nose noisily.

Then, suddenly, she began to cough. Coughs that shook her whole body and seemed almost to shake the concrete step beneath her. Her face grew crimson, then almost blue and she was choking, hardly able to breathe.

"Are you okay?" Jeff moved toward her, wondering what he should do. She shook him away.

Once more she reached into her bag and pulled out a bottle and discolored spoon. Still coughing and gagging, she shakily poured some of the brown liquid into the spoon and jammed it into her mouth.

"So? What are you staring at?"

"Nothing, I'm sorry." Jeff busied himself once more picking up the broken glass. He stood up, looking for a trash receptacle.

"Here," she said, holding out a sheet of newspaper.

"Thanks." He dropped the glass onto the paper, intending to throw it all away, but she drew back her hand and, folding the paper over the glass, put it into her shopping bag.

"Never know when it will come in handy," she said. "Ain't that right?"

"Sure," he said. "Sure."

"You think I'm crazy, don't you?"

"No, not at all."

"Liar."

For the first time in months, Jeff was beginning to enjoy himself. "You're no crazier than me."

She cocked her head. "You don't look crazy—little stupid, maybe, not crazy."

"Oh, but, you don't know. I—see things." He had meant to joke, but in the middle, the familiar chill spurted through his body. Why had he said it?

Too late. Her pale greyish eyes were glittering. "What do you see?" she asked.

He swallowed hard. Maybe if he told someone . . . "Clouds," he said, "mushroom clouds. Scares the devil out of me." He tried to smile, but his mouth stuck.

Something stirred behind the old eyes. "Like Japan? In the war?"

He nodded.

She sniffed, wiping her nose on a grubby rag. "Crazy not to be scared of that," she said.

The chill passed. He liked the woman more every minute. "Mind if I sit down?"

"I don't. The reverend highness William P. Prisspot might." She pulled her shopping bags closer to make room for him.

"The reverend who?" he asked, wishing he'd thought to sit upwind of her.

"Aw, the preacher at this so-called church. He thinks I lower the property values or something, sitting on his fancy steps. God awmighty, at least I don't break beer bottles all over them."

"I said I was sorry."

"You don't want any supper, do you?"

"What? Oh, no, thanks," he said as she brought a white MacDonald's sack from the shopping bag and took out what remained of a well-chewed hamburger.

"You'd be surprised what people throw away," she said.

"Mrs. Dodson!" The brown wooden door had opened behind them, and a man in a dark suit and blue tie was towering above them.

"Whoppedo," the old woman said through her burger. "It's neighborhood cleanup time."

The man came down the stairs and stood on the pavement in front of them, but he still seemed to be towering over them. "Mrs. Dodson, what are you doing here?"

Jeff was more surprised by the fact that the old woman had a name than by the fact that the minister knew it.

"I thought you were all settled into Friendship House."

"Oh, Preach, that place is worse than the slammer. I can't stay there. It's a bunch of eighty-year-old pickpockets and street-walkers. What's an honest old lady like me gonna do in a dump like that?"

"In the first place, Mrs. Dodson, you're about as honest as Jesse James. And in the second place, you're sick and have no business sleeping on the street in this weather."

"Well, it's your fault. If you'd let me sleep on one of them nice red-cushioned benches in there . . ."

"Mrs. Dodson, you know I can't let you do that."

"It's not as if you was crowded to the doors. You hardly got half a house Sunday morning, and you sure as Christmas don't have anybody there at night."

"It's a church, Mrs. Dodson, not a motel. Besides, it's not really up to me."

"Next you'll be telling me God won't let you."

"I'm afraid God doesn't have much to say about it. It's the church board that makes policies about the use of the building, and *they* feel you'd be much more comfortable in Friendship House."

"Well, Friendship House don't happen to suit me. I'm very sorry." She jabbed Jeff with her elbow. "That's your line, ain't it, sonny?" She put her palm on her chest and lifted her head.

"I'm sorry, reverend, so sorry, so very sorry." The old lady was an actress. He loved her.

"Would you introduce me to your friend, Mrs. Dodson?" the minister asked, interrupting her performance.

"What? Oh, the kid." She seemed to consider Jeff. "Just some crazy delinquent took up with me. Don't worry. I'll trash him before nighttime. The board wouldn't want *him* on their fancy benches."

"Does he have a name?" the minister asked, smiling at Jeff.

"Even a dog's got a name," she grumped. "I just don't happen to want to tell you. You'd ship him off to Friendship House to rot."

"Oh, come on now, Mrs. Dodson. We're only trying to help."

"Yeah, that's what the snake said to Eve."

Jeff caught the minister's eye and they both started laughing. Jeff couldn't help himself. The woman was priceless.

"You see why I let this woman drive me crazy, don't you?" the man said.

Jeff nodded. Mrs. Dodson humphed and went back to chewing at her used hamburger.

"Mrs. Dodson," the minister said, "tell you what. You go back to Friendship House just for tonight. It's going to be freezing. Just go back there this one night, and by tomorrow I'll find you another place."

"Not the slammer."

"No."

"Not the state hospital."

He raised three fingers in a salute. "Scout's honor," he said.

She pretended to consider it. "How about five dollars for a nice warm supper? This hamburger's about wore out."

"You remember what you did with the five dollars I gave you last week?"

"Cough syrup. I got this terrible cough." She coughed a bit to prove it.

The minister pulled a wallet from his pocket. He took out a five-dollar bill. The woman reached out for it, but he handed it to Jeff instead. "Would you do me a favor and take her down to the café at the corner of Fifth and Main and see that she gets some solid food in her? Now don't go pouting, Mrs. Dodson. You know what would happen to this money if I gave it to you."

She wouldn't let Jeff help carry the shopping bags. She insisted on dragging them herself the five blocks to the café. At least once on every block she fell into a fit of coughing, bending over with her rag-wrapped head nearly on the pavement.

At last he pushed open the café door and waited as she

hauled herself and her possessions the last few feet into the warmth. "Hey, Rosie," someone yelled. "I see they let you out."

"Shut up," she replied pleasantly. She was obviously at ease here. "I got money," she said to the waitress, a woman of about sixty years with the build of a linebacker, "and I'll have the special." She turned to Jeff anxiously. "You hungry?"

"No," he said.

She smiled happily. "Too bad." She settled back. "A tall draft for me, Gert. And how 'bout"—she smiled mischievously—"how 'bout a side order of mushrooms for the boy?"

He flushed and began to fiddle with the edge of the paper napkin.

The old woman leaned towards him. "Now don't let a little teasing curl your upper plate, sonny."

"It's okay," he said, not looking up. "The whole thing's pretty stupid. I know that."

"Be stupid not to be scared," she said again.

He looked up. She was smiling at him. "You really think so?"

"Sure. You never know what those Japs'll do."

He almost started to explain to her that the Japanese had nothing to do with his fears, but it seemed too complicated, so he just smiled back.

The food came. It was all the same color—a thick white

gravy covered the meat loaf and mashed potatoes, and there were white beans on the side. But she ate with enthusiasm. "Wanna bite?"

"No, thanks. My mom's expecting me."

"That's sweet," she said. "You having a mother. I figured you for a stray."

"Not quite," he said.

When she had finished, wiping the plate clean with a piece of white bread and lifting the empty glass three times to try to squeeze out another drop, she gave a big sigh and sagged back against the booth.

It was well past dusk outside. His mother would be hysterical. "How are you going to get to Friendship House?" he asked.

She looked up sharply. "It's only a couple blocks from here. I can walk her. No rush."

He hesitated.

"You better run along home. I want to just sit here for a while before committing myself to that fruit basket."

"You'll be all right?"

"Sonny, I been all right for seventy-eight years, which is more than I can say for you."

He paid Gert at the cash register. "I hope you didn't leave my tip on the table. Rosie will steal it, sure," Gert said as she took his money.

He flushed. He'd forgotten the tip, so he handed her the change. "It's from the church," he said.

"Yeah," she said. "I figured. What a bum."

"She's not a bum." Why on earth was he defending her? Of course she was a bum. But he hated the waitress for saying it. He borrowed a pencil and took a napkin off the counter and wrote his phone number on it. He walked back to the booth. "Here," he said, pulling a quarter from his pocket. "This is my phone number. In case you need somebody."

"You are crazy, ain't you?"

"Yep," he said. They both smiled.

His mother was only slightly hysterical. He pretended to be offended by her so that he wouldn't have to talk during supper. He didn't want to have to explain to her that he was late because he had been taking a bag lady out to dinner.

He went to bed, thinking more about that crazy old woman than the end of the world. But once asleep, the nightmares returned. There was the blinding flash of light. He raised his arm to shield his face and saw his own bones through the flesh. An alarm began to ring. He sat up sweating. It was the telephone.

He jumped out of bed, ran to the kitchen, and snatched it up. He was still panting.

"Sonny?"

"Who is this?"

"It's Rosie. Who's this?"

"It's me, Rosie. You woke me up."

"That's what you get for sleeping."

His mother was calling from her bedroom, asking who was on the phone. He covered the mouthpiece. "Just this girl I know, Mom. It's okay." She grumbled about telephone calls at ungodly hours, but he knew she liked the idea that some girl was calling him. Hoo haw, what a girl.

"You still there, sonny?"

He cupped his hand around the receiver and spoke as quietly as he could. "Where are you? Are you all right?"

She began to cough in answer, choking and gasping.

"Rosie? Where are you?"

"I'm in the church," she managed to gasp out. "It's cold as hades in here. I think they turned off the stinking heat." She began to cough again. "I don't feel so great," she gasped out at last.

"I'm coming," he said.

"Side door," she managed to say before another spasm of coughing.

When he got to the side door of the church, it was open. He slipped in. Except for the red glow from the exit lights, it was pitch dark. He fumbled instinctively for a switch, but realized in time that more light was sure to bring the police.

"Rosie," he called softly, feeling his way down the corridor. "Rosie, where are you?" He heard her coughing and followed the sound. He could make out the dim outline of the pulpit to his left and the pews stretching back to his right. The smell of greenery spiced the cold air. "Rosie?"

She was slumped over in a pew near the front. He felt her forehead the way his mother used to feel his when he was small.

"I don't feel so good," she said.

"I think you have a fever," he said. "Shouldn't you go to a hospital?"

"Who do you think I am, sonny, Mrs. Nelson B. Vanderbilt?"

"If you go, they gotta take you in."

"We already figured out you was crazy, right?"

He sat down beside her. Her old face glowed red from the exit light over the side entrance.

"You see things, don't you, sonny?"

"Yeah."

"Can you see if I'm gonna die tonight or not?"

The idea of her dying was like looking at his own bones through his arm. "You're not going to die, Rosie."

"I'm gonna die. Maybe not tonight. But sometime soon enough."

"Don't say that."

"You care, don't you?" She twisted around to try to look

at him. "That's kinda sweet." She settled back. "I like that."

They sat there in the silent darkness, her shoulder against his. Hers was wrapped in so many layers of clothing that there didn't seem to be a human body underneath, but there was. He knew there was.

"I'm scared, you know. I ain't been all that good. I figger God's gonna get me something awful."

He opened his mouth to reassure her, when suddenly, he saw it. A plain wooden cross hung from the beams over the pulpit, and right behind the cross, swelling up from the shadows at the back wall, the form of the terrible mushroom cloud. He punched her shoulder. "There, Rosie, you see it?"

She jerked her eyes open. "What? See what, sonny?"

"The cloud—there, right behind the cross."

"God awmighty. We're a pair." Then she hunched her shoulders and squinted. "That ain't no cloud, sonny. That's one of them fancy glass windows. Look again. That's angel's wings. See, there in the window. It's an angel."

And it was an angel. An angel bending over talking to a woman.

"Fear not." He said it out loud.

"What, sonny?"

"That's what the angel said, 'Fear not.' "

"That's sweet," she said. "I like it." She stretched out away from him on the bench, shoving him with her tennis shoes so that he stood up. She sighed. "Maybe God ain't out to get me after all. Sent me my own private angel. Might be a crazy angel, but he's sweet." She punched the air in his direction so that he would know she was joking.

Jeff took off his jacket and put it over her legs, but it was hardly enough. He went back into the hall and nosed about until he found the choir room which had a closet full of robes. He grabbed a handful from the rack and took them back to the sanctuary. He began covering her with the robes, but she seemed so quiet . . . What if she had died on him, here in this cold church? What could he do? "Rosie," he called softly. Then louder, "Rosie!"

She didn't move. All he had done was go to the choir room, and now she was dead.

"Rosie!" he called hoarsely. "Are you all right?" Oh, God, don't let her die.

The old woman opened one eye. "Fear not," she said. "Fear not, sonny. Just get my bags from the ladies room and get on home before your mother calls the cops."

He brought her bags. "Are you going to be okay?"

She snuggled under the mound of choir robes. "Sleeping in heavenly peace, sonny." She cackled. "Didn't know I knew that line, did you now?"

He patted her and took one last look at the angel over the altar. If he'd known how to pray properly he would have thanked someone. "Take care of her," he said to the angel or God or Jesus—whoever watched out for old bag ladies and crazy kids.

It was black outside, and bitter cold without his jacket. Above the darkened streets, the sky sagged under a load of stars. But there was one star far more brilliant than the rest, its light almost touching the shadows of the houses—like a flaming solitary dance low in the eastern sky.

Maybe he was seeing things again. Rosie was right. He was crazy. But this time he was not afraid.

A Ruckus

by Thacher Hurd

Hey, let's build a spaceship!

HOW THIS BOOK CAME TO BE

At a conference not very long ago, a young librarian remarked angrily that she had just come from a book-selection meeting at which some of her colleagues had enthused over a new "war" book containing numerous photographs of German tanks used during the Second World War.

"The kids will love this one," somebody said. "I'm going to buy multiple copies for my library."

"But there are no photographs in the book," our angry librarian retorted, "showing what these tanks did to people. Why do we have to keep pushing *war* in our books for children?"

Out of her anger, and the strong antiwar feeling of others in the children's book community, the idea of this big book for peace was born.

Dutton Children's Books offered to publish it, and a letter was mailed to a group of distinguished children's book authors and illustrators, asking them to contribute. We felt proud and elated that so many talented, busy people were eager to be part of this book.

Their royalties and income from the publisher's sale of the book will be donated to the following organizations to help in their work for peace:

Amnesty International

Amnesty International is a worldwide human-rights organization that works specifically for the release of prisoners of conscience, fair and prompt trials for all political prisoners, and an end to torture and executions in all cases. To become a member or for more information, write to Amnesty International, 322 Eighth Avenue, New York, NY 10001 (phone 1-800-55AMNESTY).

The Carter Center's Conflict Resolution Program (Emory University)

In thinking of peace, we often neglect the world's deadliest wars within countries' borders and outside the purview of international peace organizations. The Carter Center's Conflict Resolution Program is aimed at seeking solutions to these horrible wars. For more information, write to The Carter Center Peace Fund, P.O. Box 105515, Atlanta, GA 30307 (phone 404-331-3900).

Greenpeace

An international organization dedicated to the protection of our natural environment. Greenpeace's efforts include campaigns to stop nuclear and toxic pollution, the slaughter of species such as whales and seals, the testing and production of nuclear weapons, the arms race at sea, and the exploitation of the Antarctic continent. For more information, write to Greenpeace, 1436 U Street, N.W., Washington, D.C. 20009 (phone 202-462-1177).

The Lion and the Lamb Peace Arts Center

Providing an opportunity for the study and promotion of peace and international understanding through the arts and literature for children. For more information, write to The Lion and the Lamb Peace Arts Center, Bluffton College, Bluffton, OH 45817 (phone 419-358-8015, ext. 207).

SANE / FREEZE: Campaign for Global Security

One of the nation's largest grassroots peace and justice organizations. Its activist network stresses local involvement in programs which develop the inextricable link between peace, the environment, and economic justice for all. For more information, write to SANE / FREEZE, 711 G St., S.E., Washington, D.C. 20003 (phone 202-546-7100).

The printing and binding of this volume was generously
donated by South China Printing Company, Hong Kong.

The book was set in Galliard by PennSet, Inc.